JOHN CORIGLIANO

THREE IRISH FOLKSONG SETTINGS

for Voice and Flute

I. The Salley Gardens
II. The Foggy Dew
III. She Moved Through the Fair

duration: ca. 10 minutes

recording: RCA 60395-2-RG
Robert White, tenor, Ransom Wilson, flute

ED-3833
First Printing: July 1991

G. SCHIRMER, Inc.

DISTRIBUTED BY
HAL•LEONARD®
CORPORATION
7777 W. BLUEMOUND RD. P.O. BOX 13819 MILWAUKEE, WI 53213

ISBN 0-7935-0430-9

THREE IRISH FOLKSONG SETTINGS

Traditional Folksongs
arranged by
John Corigliano

Padraic Colum

I. The Salley Gardens

II. The Foggy Dew

Anonymous

Fast, bright, quick

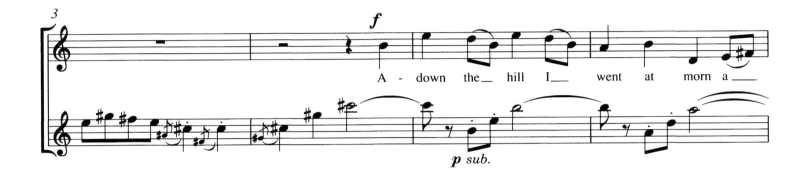

A - down the_ hill I_ went at morn a ___ love - ly_ maid I spied. Her hair was_ bright as the dew that wets sweet_

Ann - ers_ ver - dant side. "Now_ where go ye, sweet_ maid?" said I. She _

liquid

* Grace notes *on* the beat

A tempo I°

raised her __ eyes of __ blue, And smiled and __ said, "The __ boy I'll wed I'm to

meet __ in the fog - gy dew!"

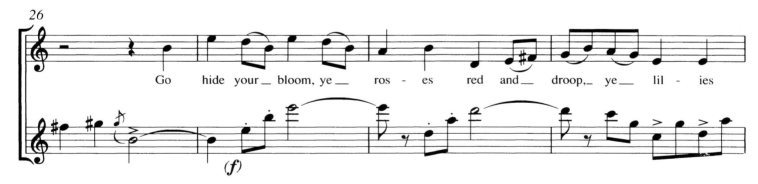

Go hide your __ bloom, ye __ ros - es red and __ droop, __ ye __ lil - ies

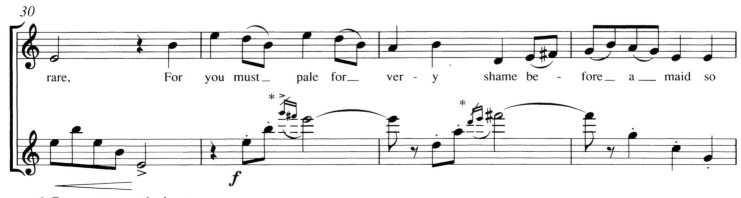

rare, For you must __ pale for __ ver - y shame be - fore __ a __ maid so

* Grace notes *on* the beat

6

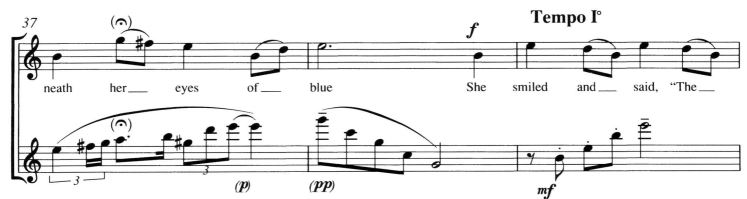

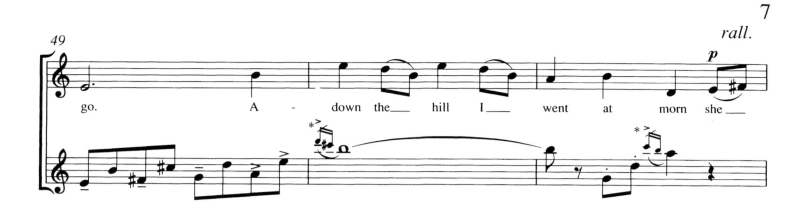

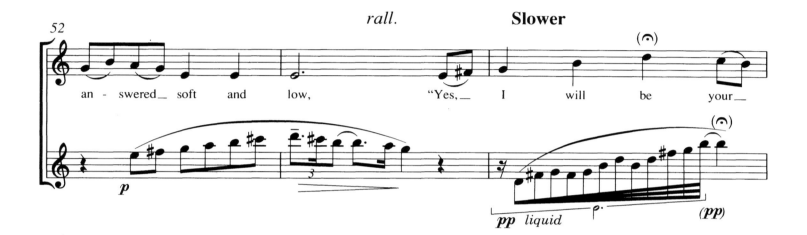

* Grace notes *on* the beat

III. She Moved Through the Fair

William Butler Yeats

And she stepped _____ a - way from me and this she did

say, "It _____ will not be long, love, _____ 'til __ our wed - ding

accel. **Slightly faster**

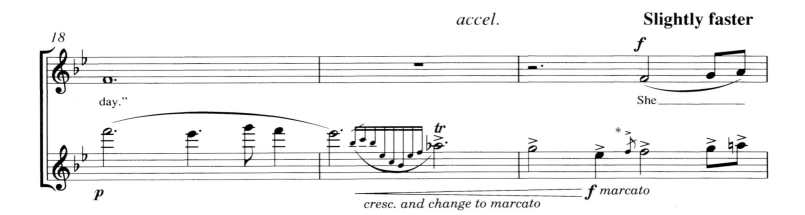

day." She _____

cresc. and change to marcato

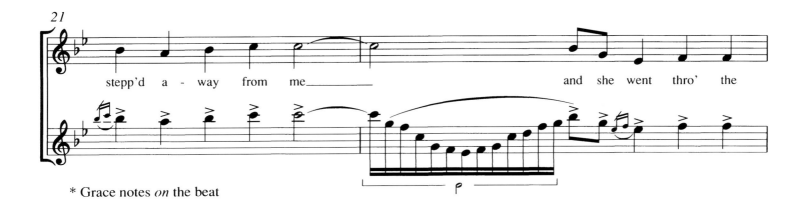

stepp'd a - way from me _____ and she went thro' the

* Grace notes *on* the beat

fair, And fond - ly_____ I watched her move here and move

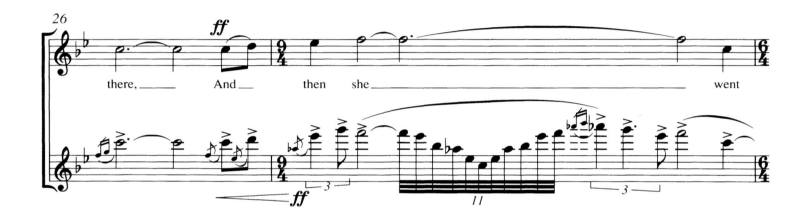

there,_____ And_ then she_____ went

home - ward with one star a - wake, As the_ swan in the eve - ning_____

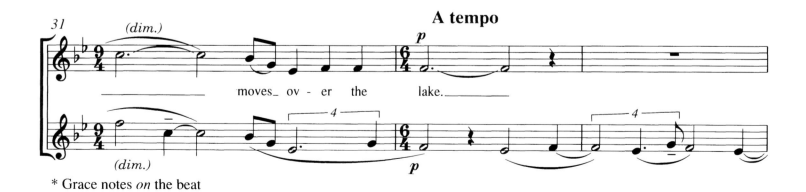

_____ moves_ ov - er the lake._____

* Grace notes *on* the beat

Last _____ night she came to me, _____ she__ came soft - ly

p dolce

in _____ So soft - ly _____ she came that her feet made no

gentle

din, _____ And she laid her _____ hand__ on me and this she did

pp gentle ⌐3⌐ ══════ *niente* *pp*

say, _____ "It ___ will not be long, love, _____ 'til__ our wed - ding

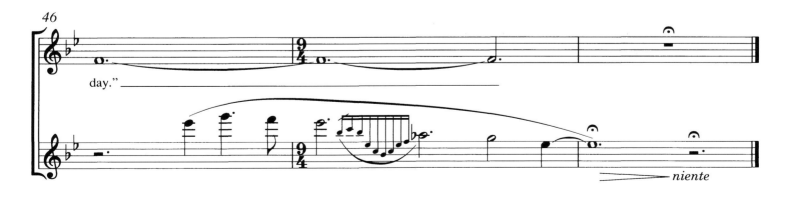

day." _____

niente